HOW TO PUNCH KIDS IN BATHROOMS

By
John Marszalkowski

Copyright © 2019 by BARF-BAG PUBLISHING

All rights reserved. This book or any portion thereof may not be reproduced or used in any manner whatsoever without the express written permission of the publisher except for the use of brief quotations in a book review or scholarly journal.

First Printing: 2019

ISBN
ebook   978-1-7320226-7-6
Paperback 978-1-7320226-8-3

BARF-BAG PUBLISHING
PO BOX 210454
MILWAUKEE WI 53221-8008
http://ThisIsAReal.Company

Ordering Information:
Special discounts are available on quantity purchases by corporations, associations, educators, and others. For details, contact the publisher at the above-listed address.

U.S. trade bookstores and wholesalers: Please contact Barf-Bag Publishing at the above-listed URL address.

HOW TO PUNCH KIDS IN BATHROOMS

By
John Marszalkowski

For Desiree:
I'm sorry that I can't shut up.

CONTENTS

You Didn't Ask But Let's Talk About Me 1

Self-No-Help. 5

Can-Cans 9

How To Punch Kids In Bathrooms. 13

Fifteen Pieces of Flair 15

I've Got A Used Car With Your Name On It 19

Acknowledgements 23

"If thou wilt make a man happy, add not unto his riches but take away from his desires."

—Epicurus

You Didn't Ask But Let's Talk About Me

Howdy, friend! I'm so glad you're reading this book. Let me introduce myself.

My name is John Marszalkowski, and I love talking about myself. I've been writing "professionally" since 2018. For most of my life, I told myself I could never write a book because I wasn't a strong reader. Only in recent years have I had the courage to write anyways.

Some might say I'm middle-aged, while others argue that I'm too young for that title. I'm most likely never going to see the year 2072.

In the year 2072, I think it's incredibly possible my wife, Desiree, will be an 87-year-old 9th-degree Grandmaster of Brazilian Jiu-Jitsu. My daughters will be 57 and 53 doing who-knows-what with their lives.

Charlotte is turning 4-years-old this year, and her interests include playgrounds, legos, drawing, Disney princesses, being outside, and her BFF Evelyn. If I had to guess today, I'd say she'll be an engineer and design roller coasters for Walt Disney World. My other daughter will be born this year, and so I know nothing about her yet. Well, she likes to kick her mom sometimes. So, a soccer player, I suppose.

I am a man who can be defined by his family. I will do anything Desiree asks me to do, so long as I'm paying attention to her when she asks and I don't forget to do whatever it is. She asks little of me, so it's pretty easy. I'm a writer because it seems like the only thing I can get done when Charlotte is glued to the TV or tablet. It's also the only job I want to do right now because I don't need to leave the house. If I don't have to leave the house, I don't need to wear pants. If you can make any amount of money without wearing pants, you've stumbled upon something special. I have no idea what effects my unborn daughter is going to have on my life, but regardless, I'm really excited to meet her and mold myself into what she needs me to be.

I've been diagnosed with Attention Deficit Disorder. I believe I was diagnosed as hyperactive as a child, but as an adult, I've become more the "inattentive" type, rather than "hyperactive." In a nutshell, I have a genetic neurological disease that makes even the smallest tasks feel overwhelming. Large tasks are usually just completely avoided, unless they are unavoidable, in which case I'll likely either have a panic attack or lay face-down on the floor and wait for death. The only way I can get anything done is to break things down into MICRO-tasks and take a lot of breaks. For the Baby Boomers and earlier, this was just called "Being A Lazy Good-For-Nothing Bum." Now it's recognized as an incurable disease. This changes nothing, however. How lazy people are defined today and the symptoms of inattentive ADHD coincidently match up perfectly.

You might enjoy this book if your brain is anything like mine. Very short chapters, constantly changing subjects, and sort of weird. And, if you do happen to enjoy this book, I have other books too (wink wink).

"Success is liking yourself, liking what you do, and liking how you do it."

—Maya Angelou

Self-No-Help

One thing I can't be clear enough about is how little I understand the universe. We all gather information and life lessons as we go along (some more than others), and I have an overwhelming urge to write about things I have come to realize. It could be that I love to teach, but it's more likely some form of pretentiousness.

Everyone is ignorant regarding almost everything. When I finally find myself believing I know the truth about something, I can't help but evangelize it. The problem is, that doesn't mean you should listen to me.

I tend to hate almost any kind of motivational writing I read. I don't know why. Perhaps it's because I'm a skeptic. A good friend of mine once asked me if I consider myself a pessimist after I undoubtedly made a glass-half-empty statement. I didn't want to say that I was, as pessimism is undoubtedly a negative quality, but I believed that I might be. After some self-reflection, I chalked it up to skepticism more than pessimism. I have information trust issues. Some of the most trusted and beloved people in my life fed me theology disguised as facts throughout my childhood. It would take me years to unlearn. I tend to put up defensive walls when I hear anything being preached to me. Even hearing confidence in someone's perspective is oddly a red flag. My reaction comes across as pessimistic, but really what I'm saying is "I don't believe you yet. Why should I?" That's not saying you're unbelievable. It's just saying that I require you to go above and beyond in convincing me you are a credible source on the subject you are talking about. Chances are, my pessimistic ass isn't worth the time and effort.

Here is where my hypocrisy is downright embarrassing: I'm not a credible source on pretty much anything.

I constantly find myself wanting to say "You know what you should do? You should…" but then I usually stop myself, because what do I know?

I also think society, or at least the types of people who get off on motivational talk, has a weird infatuation with penance, the idea that self-inflicted suffering is required to fix your problems. The mere thought of blood, sweat, and tears being shed to accomplish something really gets their rocks off. What if accomplishing that same thing could be painless and effortless? I don't know if it can always be, but I think sometimes it's possible. It's these damn physiological obstacles that have to make everything so annoying. You can't say "This is the desired result. Now do it." You might need to have mental acrobatics to get there. That's where motivational speakers and self-help authors earn their paycheck.

Anyway, the point of this chapter was to let you know where I'm at with the whole know-it-all thing. If I ever start sounding a little too ostentatious, I need you to let me know.

I don't like the feeling I get when I read it in other people's words, so I certainly don't want it to invoke that with mine.

That said, let me now tell you about how the world is, how it should be, and what you should do about it.

"There is no greater agony than bearing an untold story inside you."

—Maya Angelou

Can-Cans

In 1987, my family and I went to Walt Disney World. It was my first time, though my parents and older siblings had gone before. I was five years old and it was pretty awesome. I returned several times in my childhood. If you haven't been, I recommend it.

At Disney World, one of the attractions I was very attracted to was called The Diamond Horseshoe. It was a western-style show that involved singing cowboys and Can-Can girls. I really liked those Can-Can girls, but I had no idea why. Starting from when I was as young as five and for several years after, I would stare at the corsets that forced their bodies into inhuman hourglasses, feminine makeup, long hair, and their long-legged fishnet stockings. I would stare at them in that moment, and then daydream about them all year.

I was young and years away from puberty. I didn't know anything about sex. Yet, there was this driving cognitive urge to be as close to them as possible. What could be the most I'd hope for? Dreams of pecks on cheeks, hugs, and hand holding. But why?

I was pretty interested in the idea of naked women. I never saw one, but I sure wanted to. Even when I was five years old, I didn't know why I wanted to see them, but I knew that if I did, that would probably be the greatest thing in life that there is to see.

Of course, nudity alone wasn't the obsession, it was specific body parts. Had it been a normal rule of society for women to hide their elbows, I'd probably have been obsessed with the idea of seeing them uncovered. I was very interested in seeing the bare curves of other more mysterious areas.

However, I knew it wasn't just a fascination with the unknown. There was a drive to do something, long before any part of me would have been able to, and that was the mystery that haunted me.

I remember seeing a movie poster for "Elvira: Mistress of the Dark" in 1988 in which actress Cassandra Peterson's perfectly round breasts popped out of a neckline that left nothing to the imagination. I would find myself thinking "What if I could just stick my face right in between those things? What would that accomplish? Nothing, obviously. So why do I want to do that?"

It wasn't just the mysterious parts of women that intrigued me, but some of the most familiar. Consider hands, for example. Both men and women had hands, but men had these big, calloused meat paws. Men's hands made fists. The kind of hands that punched kids in a public bathroom. Women's hands were small, soft, and healing when caressing to console.

I wanted those Can-Can girls to caress my face. Even more, I wanted to curl up under bed sheets with them. I just had no idea why. Years later, it would all make sense. My mother gave me a "birds and the bees" talk that started with her asking me "What do you think sex is?" I replied, "When people take off their clothes and lay in a bed together and kiss." That was the most I had confirmed of the act from movie scenes before being shooed away from the TV by my parents. In response to my answer, my mother explained a very unexciting biological procedure for which a grown man plants a seed into his one and only wife for the sole purpose of making a baby.

I remember the explanation offering no answers for some questions I was too afraid to ask, such as "If boobs are just feed bags for babies, then why am I so interested in them?"

In fact, the biology lesson only explained why one part of my body would want to go anywhere near one part of a female body. It didn't explain why people kiss, for example, or why when I got older I wasn't allowed to watch "The Benny Hill Show" anymore.

Looking back on it, it's obvious for me to see that I was attracted to girls, long before puberty. But I suppose it could have been different. Instead of Can-Can girls, I could have felt that way about the cowboys. Instead of wanting to motorboat Elvira's funbags, I might have dreamt about Jean-Claude Van Damme's sweaty, chiseled torso on the movie poster for "Bloodsport." I have no idea why people are born the way they are. But I fully believe that other children experience what I did, with varying results. Sometimes society isn't as accepting of what everyone feels. I could easily tell my parents I thought the can-can girls were pretty. How many boys had to bury their infatuations for the cowboys? I'm guessing almost all of them.

"This particular event happened last summer on my uncle's farm in Virginia. My brother and I had just finished cutting a field of hay and were enjoying the evening meal under the shade of an elm tree. He went down for water by the creek and while he was gone, I took a bowl that was filled with delicious plum pudding and placed into it, not one, but two large pieces of sheep shit. When he returned I encouraged him to taste the plum pudding, and as sure as I'm standing before you today, he did! He ate it all! Shit pudding! He ate shit pudding!

...And to be completely honest sir, I have no brother. It was me. I ate sheep shit! I swear I did!"

—*Steven M. Porter*

How To Punch Kids In Bathrooms

When I was about eight years old, I was pretty interested in drawing. At that time it was mostly doodles of the Teenage Mutant Ninja Turtles. My mother thought I might have some talent, or at least enough interest to warrant paying for art classes at the Milwaukee Art Museum.

I along with about nine other kids my age gathered in a large room. We had a teacher who was a very nice woman. The bathroom was down the hall slightly, just across from the elevators.

One day when I went to the bathroom, an old man followed me in. I used the urinal and he stayed near the door, by the sink. When I finished and turned around, he came at me bouncing like a boxer, throwing jabs. I was hit and fell back onto the floor. I don't really remember all the details from that point on. What I do remember is laying on the floor motionless as he then went on to phantom box himself in the mirror before walking out. The next thing I remember is my teacher touching my face and yelling for someone to call security. The last detail I remember is standing next to my mother, as security guards explained to her that he was "probably a homeless man with dementia."

That was the last I remember of art classes.

I was too scared to use a public bathroom or an elevator alone for a few years after that, but the fear faded away in time.

I'm sure I'm not the first kid to have this happen. There is no moral to this story. Sometimes crazy old homeless guys beat up small boys in public bathrooms and get away with it.

I'm not bitter.

It's fine.

I'm fine.

Fifteen Pieces of Flair

There is a scene in the 1999 movie "Office Space," where Jennifer Aniston's character, a waitress at a kitschy restaurant chain, is reprimanded by her supervisor for wearing only fifteen pieces of flair, the bare minimum (flair, in this case, being goofy buttons). He compares her to her coworker who wears thirty-seven pieces of flair. She asks her boss a valid question: "If you want me to wear thirty-seven pieces of flair, then why don't you just make the minimum thirty-seven pieces of flair?"

I don't see what's so wrong with bare minimums, honestly. They are set for a reason, and if you can meet the parameters of those expectations, what's the problem?

People have this weird obsession with "giving 110%." I'm not sure where this came from, probably a competitive environment growing up, or something. But anything over 100% is impossible, so that's just bad math.

I do understand countersteering to correct a slide in the wrong direction. For example, if a squirrel needs a bare minimum amount of nuts to survive the winter, it would be in its best interest to bury more than that amount, as it will likely forget where some of them are hidden. The squirrel needs to hoard in order to offset the inevitable missing inventory. If the squirrel fails to do this, the consequences are extreme.

However, if the squirrel likes to take risks, and has an amazing memory, the bare minimum is enough. That's why it's the minimum. It's just barely enough, but it's enough.

This book is the bare minimum. I wanted to see how short of a book I could make but still get a message across. The point is simple: I write books that are kind of like this one. Once I've written what I think is enough content to capture the vibe of my writing style, I'll have buried enough nuts to survive the winter. I'll have shown you whether or not you might want to read my other books. What can I say? I'm a squirrel that likes to take risks when it comes to writing. At least I'm transparent about my intentions.

I wanted to fill around 32 pages with rants and rambles. Why 32 pages? Because that's the minimum for some printers. As an eBook this could have been as short as a single page, but since some people prefer paper in hand, I wanted to make sure I covered all the bare minimum requirements. Some printers only require 18 pages. Since I'm not sure who I'm going to be printing with, I need to over-correct for the unknown. I still do the bare minimum, but I choose the highest minimum.

I believe in overcorrecting to eliminate risks in life. Better to buy an extra loaf of bread and have extra food than to not buy enough and go hungry. Better to earn more money than you spend, so you can save for unexpected expenses. Better to exceed people's expectations just slightly, than to leave them unimpressed.

When it comes to others giving you a bare minimum, it is their burden to clearly communicate their expectations. If you tell me the minimum is fifteen pieces of flair, I have to assume that's the amount you want.

And if you're an employer, and you don't think your employee is worth a nickel over the bare minimum wage, you don't deserve more than the minimum pieces of flair.

This is why I don't expect a cashier at Walmart to smile or be nice to me. Why should they? In 2018, the average employee wage there was $9/hour and their CEO made $10,961/hour.

"No, we're not homosexual, but we are willing to learn."

—*Harold Ramis*

I've Got A Used Car With Your Name On It

The "Call To Action" is an advertising phrase that basically asks a person to do something, such as "click here" or "call now." I'd be doing a terrible job if I didn't take this opportunity to tell you about my other books, ask for reviews, and beg for you to share your thoughts with others. I will try as hard as I can to not sound like a used car salesman.

My first book is titled **BUY MY BOOK: *Not Because You Should, But Because I'd Like Some Money*.** I would now describe it as a collection of informal essays, but honestly, I don't think it fits into any category or genre. I called it a memoir at the time, but that's a misleading description. My goal was to make a book of random nonsense that also touched on ideas that are important to me. I basically tried to make the kind of book I wish existed; an ADHD dream come true for weirdos and possibly a nightmare for everyone else. I'm told it's funny, but I'm not confident enough to make that claim. So far it has been scoring high reviews on Goodreads and Amazon if you want to check it out. You can order the paperback or hardcover from virtually any bookstore (check out indiebound.org to find an indie bookstore near you). There is also an audiobook version available on Audible and iTunes. The eBook is available almost everywhere eBooks are sold.

It's hard to say if **HOW TO PUNCH KIDS IN BATHROOMS** (the book you're currently reading) is technically my second book or not. Technically I've written this book after finishing what would have been my second book, titled **UNCREDIBLE THOUGHTS: Essays, Spiels, and Poppycock**. I think I'll be publishing *HOW TO PUNCH KIDS IN BATHROOMS* first so that I can inform you now that *UNCREDIBLE THOUGHTS* will be available in November of 2019. It features more essays of the same style, but also a couple of attempts at fiction. Some poppycock, but overall a little more straightforward than *BUY MY BOOK*. I like to think that writing *BUY MY BOOK* was a learning experience, and *UNCREDIBLE THOUGHTS* is a result of what I learned.

I plan to continue writing more books. You'll see those publications in the same places as the books listed above.

I know I mentioned a few different sites and retailers so far, but everything is also accessible from a single link, which is for BARF-BAG PUBLISHING. That URL is…

http://ThisIsAReal.Company/

I want to thank you so much for reading this book. If you've made it here, you've read the whole thing. I don't expect most people to get here, and that makes you a very special person to me. I hope we can stay in touch for years to come.

THE END

Acknowledgements

I'd like to thank these invaluable designers for wasting their time:
- Mark Lalumondier, book designer
- Jason Gierl, cover designer

I'd like to thank these outstanding individuals for proofreading this pile of garbage:
- Matty Jay
- Kenneth Uzquiano
- Rex Tomball

I'd like to thank Will Sutton for his illustrations. I paid him for them, but I'm thankful he didn't charge me more than he did.

www.ingramcontent.com/pod-product-compliance
Lightning Source LLC
Chambersburg PA
CBHW021639080526
44584CB00015BA/1609